the potty training

Survival guide

your ultimate potty training handbook

Allison Jandu

potty expert and author of *How Do You Poo*

For every tireless hero navigating the
delightful chaos of toddlerhood

Consultant editor: Lauren Nowack
Photography courtesy of © Kelli Dirks

ISBN: Print 978-1-7369601-3-4 | eBook 978-1-7369601-4-1

Contents

Meet the Author

Hi! My name is Allison Jandu, and I am the owner and founder of Potty Training Consultant, a business that has proudly helped thousands of families reach their potty training goals and has saved more than 10 million diapers worldwide! Thank you for choosing me as your tour guide through the daunting, yet delightful, jungles of potty training! To be able to share in this experience with you is a true honor.

While I am a full-time business owner, my number one job and true passion is being the mother of my own two kids, Evan and Layla. When I potty trained them many years ago, I experienced first hand the lack of reliable resources available to parents who were having a hard time potty training. That's when I decided to become a trusted resource for other parents and caregivers in the same boat.

My mind has always worked like a scientist; I want to know the research and the why behind things. That is one of the reasons I earned my Bachelor of Science degree in Forensic Studies from the University of Baltimore back in 2006. Since then, I have spent over 5,000 hours researching all things potty training, early childhood development, human behavior and psychology – all of the factors that go into shaping a healthy potty training experience - and I'm continuing that education all the time.

In addition to my hands-on experience of working with families, each with their own unique circumstances, I have created a platform where parents can come together in a judgment-free zone, ask those hard questions, and get evidence-based solutions to tackle this challenging and amazing milestone in toddlerhood. As you dive into this book, please engage with this community so we can all encourage each other!

Join the Support Group!

Would you feel better about potty training with a team of experts in your back pocket? Join our affordable community today to be connected with the PTC team and other potty training parents for added peace of mind and support as you tackle this stage with your little one!

Scan the QR Code above to join the Potty Training Support Group - accessible via the web and right from your phone in our new mobile app! Billed as a monthly subscription. Cancel anytime.

chapter one

you've come to the right place

I'VE TITLED THIS BOOK THE POTTY TRAINING SURVIVAL GUIDE BECAUSE I KNOW FIRST HAND THAT POTTY TRAINING CAN BE DAUNTING. THERE IS NO ONE-SIZE-FITS-ALL WAY TO GET THE JOB DONE. EVERY CHILD IS DIFFERENT, AND THEREFORE, EVERY POTTY TRAINING JOURNEY IS GOING TO BE DIFFERENT TOO.

How to use this book

This book is going to give you all the tools to come out successful – and diaper-free – on the other side. If you are a visual or auditory learner, pair this book with my online, self-guided *Potty Training Survival Guide* course for audio and video resources as well. Scan the QR code to the right and use coupon WATCHANDLEARN at checkout to save 25%! Each of these programs will give you the same tools that have already helped thousands of families ditch the diapers.

By making potty training more manageable for you and your child, you are more likely to see it through to the end. Clear tools and an encouraging community keep your commitment strong, which in turn helps your child through this big transition. You'll see this theme again and again throughout this book.

To make the most of this book, please take advantage of its questions, outlines, and charts found at the end of each chapter to fully customize your process to match your family's needs and to make your potty training experience the best it can be. If you find yourself needing more assistance, reach out to schedule a custom consultation, where my team will create a specific potty plan based on your lifestyle, values, child's personality, and more.

ACKNOWLEDGING THE DIFFICULTIES OF POTTY TRAINING UPFRONT

If you're reading this, you may be feeling hesitant, excited, and nervous about potty training all at the same time. These feelings are all completely expected!

Most parents look forward to not having to change dirty diapers anymore, but the potential mess and inconvenience of the potty training process feels daunting and scary. You may be worrying about your child having an accident at the library and how you'll clean it up, if the bathroom will be clean at Chick-Fil-A when you go, or if they are going to poop on your brand new beige couch...the list of completely valid potty training concerns can go on and on.

Another tough aspect of potty training that hit me personally is that it symbolizes your baby growing up. You're essentially teaching them to be more independent, and this will be one less thing that they need you for. On top of this, most parents start potty training around the time children go through a developmental leap that comes with personality changes. This means resistance, power struggles, even tantrums as your child explores a newfound sense of autonomy and tries to do things on their own terms.

There's no question that potty training comes with its own set of challenges, but that's why you're here. We will tackle them together. But first, let's consider the more exciting parts of potty training.

LOOKING ON THE BRIGHT SIDE...

Potty training is an incredible opportunity to bond with your child. I initially fell in love with potty training when I was training my kids because, even though it was hard at times, I could see those gears turn and their eyes light up as they started having successes. Being able to be a part of that and celebrate with them was - and still is - such a rewarding aspect to parenting.

I also love potty training because it makes you slow down for a couple of days. It forces you to put the busyness of regular life on hold so you can connect with your child and get in some great quality time! You don't necessarily have to be stuck at home for an extended period of time, but it makes the process more enjoyable for everyone if you have a few, special activities planned to do while at home. This could look like special crafts, new puzzles, fun games, baking treats, watching movies, or creating sensory bins and scavenger hunts together.

Mindset shift!

Instead of looking at potty training like something you HAVE to do with your child, look at it as something you GET to do with your child. Seeing them master this newfound independence is one of the most rewarding things to experience as a parent or caregiver.

GETTING THE RIGHT MINDSET

When I'm working with a family one-on-one, I always take some time to make sure they have the right mindset and realistic expectations as they are embarking (or for some, re-embarking) on the journey.

First, **do not compare your experience to anyone else's.** Parents rarely talk about how challenging potty training is! Every child is unique, and therefore, every potty training experience will be unique as well. Some children adapt to change easily and the process comes more naturally to them, while others might struggle with transition and require more ongoing teaching and support. How things go is not a reflection on you, your parenting, or your child. **Remember, you are doing an incredible job, and I'm glad you're here.**

Second, **avoid putting a timeframe or deadline of completion on the process.** All this talk of the very popular "3-day potty training" that's out there nowadays could be setting you up for unrealistic expectations. Even though it is possible to lay the foundation for new potty habits within a very short period of time, **your child will most likely not be fully potty trained in three days** because

potty training is a process, not a one time event.

This process is going to have good and bad days, and that is normal and expected. Look for any signs of progress and focus on those. Do not measure yourself or your child by the number of accidents, but by your child's understanding of this new skill. Mistakes will be made along the way, and - believe it or not - that is when the most learning is taking place!

Lastly, **success looks different for everyone.** It's not always about pee and poop getting in the potty. For some kids, they need to start with simply getting comfortable sitting on the potty or releasing without a diaper on. Keep these things in mind as you are in the potty training trenches, and it should help you feel more confident and committed.

Apply the knowledge

Date: 8 /22 /24

Potty training means your child is growing up, becoming more independent and, very likely, experimenting with their independence and autonomy. Take a moment to write down anything that may be holding you back from potty training or making you nervous about this next step, as well as what you're looking forward to about potty training.

Your feelings about potty training:	Things that I'm nervous about:
excited Nervouse worried messy	ness, I'll not getty it. Stubborn. Failure What parts are you looking forward to? Bonding. All my attention on her. Excited. Proud.

Potty Training Activities	List some activities your child would enjoy for the first few days of potty training:
	Reading, coloring, stickers, cars, legos, trains, video

chapter two

when to start

Before we dive into the potty training itself, we need to determine the ideal time to start this process. There are a lot of factors that influence the best time to start potty training. These include:

- Your child's developmental readiness
- Other changes or transitions happening around the same time
- YOUR readiness

YOUR CHILD'S SIGNS OF READINESS

Before you start potty training, you want to make sure your child is physically, cognitively, and emotionally ready for this new phase. By waiting to start until your child is displaying some or all of these signs, the process is more likely to go smoothly. Some readiness signs are more obvious than others while others are a bit trickier to pick up on.

Research tells us that the best time to start potty training is generally around a child's second birthday, which is when most children are developmentally ready and physiologically capable of understanding and executing the skills needed to use the potty instead of a diaper. Obviously, there are a lot of different variables that come into play which could push that ideal age window one way or another. Therefore, instead of putting so much focus on age alone, I encourage families to think about developmental readiness.

According to scholar Mia E. Lang "...potty training is a very complex skill integrating physiological and behavioral processes." So, depending on a child's development, potty training is going to happen at different ages for different kiddos, and that is OKAY! Don't listen to people that make you feel like you somehow failed if you waited to start potty training until your child was older. The truth is, it's never too late to start potty training. The important thing is that you are here now and ready to get started.

Some of the main things that should be present in order to begin potty training are:

- **A good grasp on gross motor skills like sitting, standing, and walking so your child can access the potty safely.** Ultimately, the goal is for your child to use the potty independently, and if they can't safely walk there, sit down, and stand back up when they're done, then we should wait for these things to develop first. Interestingly, I have found that children who hit these gross motor milestones later tend to be ready for potty training later. Some children have physical disabilities and may not be at this point now or ever, and that is okay too. Their journey will simply look different.

- **The ability to communicate their needs and understand requests.** Your child doesn't have to be verbal yet, but they do need to be able to communicate in some way when they need to use the potty. Additionally, they should be able to understand simple requests from you. Generally, kids who are delayed with speech, language, and communication are also delayed with starting potty training. Non-verbal children are fully capable of potty training, and there are different tools that can be implemented to help them learn, just like everyone else.

- **Showing awareness or curiosity about other people's behavior.** Has your child tried to mimic what you are doing, such as walking the dog, washing the dishes, sweeping a mess, or getting dressed? This desire to be like you can be used to your advantage because if they know you use the potty, they will want to as well. You might find your child wanting to take a turn sitting on the toilet or sitting on their own floor potty nearby while you go. This is a great learning opportunity!

- **Bowel and bladder maturity.** The American Academy of Pediatrics recommends potty training around a child's second birthday because most children have enough bowel and bladder maturity by this time to successfully potty train. It wouldn't be fair to a child to ask them to use the potty if their bodies aren't physically ready. A child ready to potty train should be able to keep their diaper dry for an hour or more during the day, and some kids might even start waking up dry from naps or overnight, although that isn't a requirement to get started.

- **Consolidated daytime bowel movements.** As kids grow, they typically stop pooping during the night. Instead, they will have consolidated their poops into one or two predictable movements per day or just after they wake up. You likely know what time of day they tend to go or at least how frequently they go. If you haven't noticed any patterns yet, I have a spot at the end of this chapter for you to start taking notes about wet and soiled diapers.

Potty-Specific Signs of Readiness

THESE NEXT FEW READINESS SIGNS DON'T HAVE TO
BE PRESENT IN ORDER TO START THE PROCESS, BUT IF
THEY ARE, IT'S A GREAT BONUS.

- **Your child starts to show interest in the bathroom, toilet, toilet paper, and their own bodily functions.** Your child may start following you into the bathroom when you go, ask questions, play with the toilet paper, flush the toilet, put things into the toilet, and so on. They may try to take their diaper off after they've peed or pooped or even play with their poop or private parts. While our first instinct is to get upset because we think it is gross or inappropriate, your child is actually learning and exploring. These behaviors, while frustrating, are very normal and are great conversation starters for what those body parts are, what they do, and what comes out of them. Obviously, keep the explanations simple and age-appropriate and try not to overreact as that can unintentionally make the behavior happen more often.

- **Your child understands and communicates about having peed or pooped in their diaper.** Your child might tell you while they are peeing or pooping in their diaper or they might ask to have their diaper changed when it's wet or soiled. For children who aren't verbal, this could look like tugging at a full diaper, indicating some form of discomfort, or grabbing a new diaper and bringing it to you. Each of these examples shows an increased level of body awareness and urge recognition.

- **Hiding to poop.** A great sign that your child is ready to start potty training is if they hide when they're having a bowel movement or if they become sensitive to your presence when they are trying to go or have just gone. This could look like hiding behind the couch, covering their face in the corner, yelling at you to stay away from them, not wanting to be touched until they're done pooping, or resisting diaper changes afterwards. Why is this a good thing? It shows that they know they need to go, that they recognize the urge in their body, and they take a certain action before it happens. If they can move to their favorite hiding spot before letting their poop come out, then in theory, they can move to the potty instead.

Now remember, this isn't a checklist that needs to be marked off before you can begin the process. In fact, you can start introducing the concept of the potty to your child as young as you'd like. It's much better if you can familiarize your child and provide some positive, stress-free exposure at as young of an age as possible so that it is less of a huge transition later on. Keep reading, because we will explore some ways to do exactly that in Chapter 4.

Apply the knowledge

✓ They have a good grasp on their gross motor skills (sitting, standing, walking, etc.)

✓ They have some communication skills. They can tell me their basic needs and understand simple directions.

✓ They're imitating some of the things I do, have a new desire to be independent with certain tasks, or seem eager for positive recognition.

✓ They are able to keep a diaper dry for at least an hour or more.

? They are waking up dry from naps or overnight sometimes.

? They have predictable times when they poop and no longer poop overnight.

✓ They have a general interest in the bathroom or their bodily functions.

✓ They communicate when they are peeing or pooping, ask for a diaper change, or seem uncomfortable in a soiled diaper.

✓ They hide to poop.

Over the next few days, write down the times you changed a wet diaper and when you changed a soiled diaper on the chart below to understand your child's potty habits and routines before you get started with the training process.

	TIMES YOU CHANGE A WET DIAPER	TIMES YOU CHANGE A POOP DIAPER
DAY 1		
DAY 2		
DAY 3		
DAY 4		
DAY 5		
DAY 6		
DAY 7		
DAY 8		
DAY 9		
DAY 10		

chapter three

timing it right

Timing is everything...

You'll hear me say this a lot, but children are creatures of habit. They thrive on routine and knowing what to expect. Potty training is a major transition for a child, so we want to limit the amount of big changes that happen at the same time. Consider asking yourself this question: does potty training make sense for our family right now?

You want to be sure that, if possible, there are no other major changes or transitions happening within your family when you start to potty train. These could look like:

- Welcoming home a new baby
- Moving to a new home
- Going through a divorce
- Starting school for the first time
- Switching from a crib to a toddler bed
- Weaning from the bottle or pacifier

Any type of change or disruption in your child's life has the potential to cause emotional stress, which can lead to regressive behavior, power struggles, or meltdowns when they are faced with too much at one time. If things are already being disrupted due to another life change, it isn't setting them up for success if you throw potty training on top of it.

I recommend leaving a six to eight week buffer period between a major life change and potty training. Keep in mind that if your child is a little more sensitive, this might need to be increased. But overall, we just want things to settle down and to create a new routine for one change before moving on to the next.

MAKE SURE **YOU** ARE READY!

We often talk about a child's readiness to potty train, but a parent's readiness is just as important as you take on the role of potty coach. We already spoke about being in the right mindset as you enter this process and keeping your expectations realistic, and now we want to make sure you and your village are prepared.

Potty training affects the entire family or caregiving team as a whole. The initial part of potty training can be messy, inconvenient, stressful, tiring, and full of challenges and setbacks. Having a plan in place for how to tackle this as a team before you begin will help ensure that you remain confident and committed and come out successful on the other side.

COORDINATING WITH YOUR VILLAGE

It takes a village to raise a child, and it takes that same village to potty train effectively! If your child has a nanny, attends daycare or preschool, or has a family member that helps to care for them on a regular basis, it is strongly recommended that you chat with that team before you formally remove diapers. Having consistency with all caregivers across all environments is extremely important in helping your child learn. In addition, daycares and preschools often have rules or requirements when it comes to potty training. You want to find out what these things are before starting so you can incorporate them into how you will do things at home too.

Ask your child's care provider questions like:

- **Is potty training supported in my child's classroom?** Sometimes your child has to be in a certain age-level classroom to receive potty access. For example, if you want to start before your child turns two but the daycare doesn't allow them to use the potty yet, it's probably best to wait until they are older before pulling the plug on diapers at home to maintain consistency and avoid confusion.

- **How does using the potty in the classroom work?** Some schools have set times that every child lines up to use the potty, some schools do it on an as-needed basis only, while some schools require that a child be fully self-sufficient with their potty use from self initiation all the way through wiping and redressing.

- **What is the accident policy?** Most schools are fairly accommodating as far as changing a child when they have an accident. However, some require that a child be put back into pull ups if they have a certain number of accidents, they might request that you come in to change your child or send them home for the day, or they might require that your child remain in pull ups while at school until they can prove to be accident free for a certain number of days.

Most daycares and preschools are excited and well equipped to help your child succeed with using the potty. But, it is a team effort that requires a lot of communication. For all the families with kiddos who attend childcare, we will be talking more about how to survive this balance throughout the rest of the book.

Apply the knowledge

Our family's recent changes	Changes that have occurred in the last six months: Upcoming changes:

Possible timeframes	When are some good timeframes that make sense to start potty training?

If your child attends daycare or preschool, ask the following questions:

Is potty training supported in my child's classroom?   **YES**   **NO**

How does using the potty in the classroom work?

_____

_____

What is the accident policy?

_____

_____

chapter four

preparations

~~~~~~

PREPARATION IS ESSENTIAL TO ACHIEVING POTTY TRAINING SUCCESS ON THE FIRST ATTEMPT.

Diving into a huge change like this without a plan can lead to challenges like resistance, power struggles, and potty anxiety. We want your child to feel prepared for entering into this transition as they say goodbye to diapers and hello to the potty.

Introducing the concept of potty training, providing exposure to the toilet and bathroom, and normalizing our bodily functions from as young of an age as possible all contribute to your child being comfortable starting with an open mind and minimal fear, resistance, or uncertainty. The goal is to get them on board with the potty in fun, low-pressure ways that don't force them to do or change anything themselves right off the bat. It should feel like something that you are doing WITH your child, not TO your child.

This chapter is devoted to talking about things you can start doing **right now** to make your eventual potty training journey easier. Potty prep is going to look different for every family, but I would recommend doing at least some, if not all, of the following activities for at least two weeks before ditching the diapers.

MODEL TOILETING BEHAVIORS

Modeling toileting behaviors is the best place to start teaching your child about what happens in the bathroom. For many parents, kids are already in the bathroom when you're in there, so you might as well make it a teaching moment!

Each time you use the bathroom throughout the day, invite your child along. Say, "Oh, Mommy's body is telling her it's time to go potty!" and ask them to keep you company, tell you a story, or sing you a song while you sit. While you're doing your business, talk through the different steps. Here is an example:

"First, I have to push down my pants and underwear. Then I can sit down. I might have to wait a second sometimes for the pee and poop to come out, but I sit and make sure it's all out of my body so I feel better. Then, I can grab some toilet paper, wipe my bottom, and pull my pants and underwear back on. Then comes the really fun part – flushing! And we can't forget to wash our hands too!"

As you do this a few times, you can start involving your child more and ask them what step comes next. See if they are able to participate by handing you some toilet paper, helping flush, or pumping soap into your hands. These things not only teach them the steps of using the potty, but they also get them comfortable with the process and bathroom itself.

If your child seems comfortable, place a small floor potty in the bathroom near the toilet and invite your child to sit while you're sitting. They might start mirroring your actions. Alternatively, you can offer them a turn to sit on the toilet after you've gone. Just remember that for now, you are following their lead. So, if they say "no", do not push it any further. Instead, just say, "Okay, maybe next time."

INCORPORATE VISUAL LEARNING THROUGH VIDEOS AND BOOKS

One of my absolute favorite ways to introduce new concepts to kids is through books. Kids are very visual learners, and there are so many great potty training books in the world. Reading books about using the bathroom to kids is a great way to introduce the concept and get them familiar with it in a low-pressure, stress-free way.

When choosing a potty book, look for engaging illustrations that show all different aspects of potty use. Choose a variety of books, from simple, step-by-step picture books to silly books or ones with flaps to lift or buttons to press. Each day, incorporate at least one potty book and rotate them to keep things fresh. This will plant the potty training seed in a seamless way.

Similar to potty books, potty videos are a great way to help your child learn about potty training. If your child has a certain amount of screentime each day, make one of the videos they watch about the potty. This helps pique your child's interests about the potty, but they don't necessarily realize they're learning because they're watching a video. It's a win-win! Make sure to preview the video first to ensure it is age-appropriate, just as you would with any other online content.

Visual tools are also helpful for children who have autism or other developmental delays or disabilities.

If your child isn't verbal yet or struggles with communication, look up printable potty charts or task schedules that show each step of potty use. Some parents like to print and laminate one of these to keep in the bathroom. When you're working on modeling, especially if you have a child who isn't super verbal yet, they can point to the step in the process that comes next.

Additionally, social stories are commonly used with children who have autism to explain new concepts. A social story is a visual tool that helps children with autism understand certain situations in a very literal way. It can be as simple as a handmade book with photographs of your child and your bathroom, mixed in with some graphics of a child that resembles your child doing each step of the potty process. Seeing themselves in a story is a great way to spark interest and help them understand these new behaviors.

Flash cards are also helpful for children who struggle with speech, language, or communication. Being able to use a flash card for when they want to use the potty versus the regular toilet, need to poop or pee, or choose between reward options can help your child communicate their choices to you about their potty use. Offer choices like this whenever you can during this process to encourage independence and cooperation.

"Play is really the work of childhood."

-Fred Rogers

INTRODUCE THE POTTY THROUGH PURPOSEFUL PLAY

Playfulness is a child's love language, and it is scientifically proven to be one of the most effective ways for them to learn. So, any way you can incorporate play into the learning process is going to be beneficial and, most likely, very well received by your kiddo.

The easiest way to do this during the potty learning process is by using a drink and wet doll. Give the doll some water with its bottle, then let it sit on the potty and pee it out. Be sure to celebrate the doll's success! Not only does this help the child learn the mechanics of the body – as in, when liquid goes in, it makes pee come out – but it also allows them to see that using the potty can be fun and that the doll received a really positive response. Don't have a drink and wet doll? No problem! You can use any of your child's favorite toys or stuffed animals, and designate a small bowl for their "potty." Either way, this modeling will hopefully make your child want to try it too. It also gives your child a certain level of control over the process because it can be refreshing for them to be the teacher instead of the one being taught for a change!

As your child actually starts potty training, they can have the doll or toy as their "potty buddy", meaning someone or something that accompanies them to the potty, transitions to underwear at the same time, and to celebrate with! This way, they won't feel like the only one in the family going through this change.

MAKE POSITIVE POOP ASSOCIATIONS

Without meaning to, we sometimes use words that can unintentionally make our children feel shame or embarrassment when changing their diaper. Societal expectations are pretty much that pooping isn't something you talk about, but rather something to be kept private. Kids pick up on this from a very young age when they see us going into the bathroom and closing the door when we need to poop ourselves or our making comments about how stinky or gross poop can be. To help reverse this potential pitfall, try to shift your language while around the bathroom and dirty diapers to highlight that this is a natural, healthy process that happens to everyone, everyday.

Clinical trial findings published in 2003* showed that parents who eliminated negative terms for feces and offered praise for pooping shortened the overall amount of time for their child to potty train by about three months. So starting right now, whenever your child poops, shift your language from, "Pee-ew! Let's get you out of that stinky dirty diaper!" to "Whoa that was a big poop! I bet your belly feels so much better now!" This will help your child stop hiding when they need to poop so they can become more comfortable doing it on the potty or asking for help when they need to go. The goal here is to normalize pooping so they can see it as just another part of everyday life.

*Taubman B, Blum NJ, Nemeth N. Stool toileting refusal: a prospective intervention targeting parental behavior. Arch Pediatr Adolesc Med. 2003 Dec;157(12):1193-6. doi: 10.1001/archpedi.157.12.1193. PMID: 14662573.

THE COUNTDOWN TO POTTY TRAINING

Children are creatures of habit that thrive on predictability and knowing what to expect.

So, in most cases, children handle transitions better when they have advanced notice. For example, when they have been playing at the playground and it's time to leave, if you simply tell them, "Play time over, we have to go", your child will likely resist or even have a full on meltdown. However, if you were to say, "It's almost time for us to go. Please choose two more things to do, and then we will get in the car," your child is now involved in the timing of the departure. So, when their two things are done and you say, "That was the last thing, now it's time to go," they are more likely to comply with your request. There may still be some resistance, but you did give them fair warning and their reaction will be smaller. Let's apply this concept to potty training.

If you were to wake up one random morning and decide to get rid of the diapers, it's instantly going to cause your child's defenses to go up, which will likely create a lot of pushback. However, if you give them advanced notice that the diapers are going to disappear, they can mentally prepare. Since saying goodbye to diapers is a bigger transition than using the playground, I typically recommend making the countdown between three and five days long.

Little kids generally can't comprehend the concept of time, so try something more visual. Make a paper chain and tear off a link each night before bed, print a calendar and "x" off the days each morning, or you can have a stack of diapers in the bathroom representing the number of days that are left. As the boxes are marked off, the chain is shortened, or the diaper stack dwindles, your child has a great visual representation of the change that is coming. This also gives you an opportunity to talk to them and prepare them for how things will be different. Use this opportunity to empower them while encouraging them to ask questions and work through any feelings of hesitation or fear. Keep in mind that you have to be ready to commit at the end of this count down period. This timeline is preparing them for the lack of diapers, but also gives them a chance to see you setting a clear boundary for using the potty. Mentally prepare YOURSELF to stick with that boundary as much as possible also!

ORDER YOUR POTTY TRAINING SUPPLIES

Before Day One of potty training arrives, you'll want to have all your potty training supplies ready and waiting. This includes:

- Your potty or potties of choice

- Cleaning supplies (stain removers, disinfectants, & laundry detergent)

- New underwear

- Mattress & furniture protection

- Reward options

- Potty time activities

- A travel potty

- Potty Training On-The-Go Survival Kit

We'll cover how to pick each of these items in a little bit, but I've included a handy shopping list at the end of the chapter that you can cut out and take to the store with you, or simply scan this QR code to find a great selection of my favorite potty training essentials in my Amazon Storefront.

CHOOSING A POTTY, THE TOILET, OR BOTH

The main potty training supply you're going to need is, obviously, a potty! There are so many different options out there, it can be confusing or overwhelming to decide which one is best. Should you go with a small floor potty or skip that step and go straight to the toilet since that's the end goal anyway? Well, that depends. In most cases, I recommend starting out with a combination of both so you can take advantage of the benefits of both! In reality, there is no right or wrong answer as long as you are choosing something that your child and your family are comfortable with. So, let's explore the pros and cons of using a floor potty versus the regular toilet.

Pros of Using a Floor Potty

- Convenience. A floor potty can be moved around easily and kept within arms' reach, especially for those first few days without diapers. This is incredibly convenient so you do not have to run all the way to the bathroom with your child as they are first learning. Additionally, when you're ready to venture out, it can be kept right in the car for easy pottying on the go.

- Size. It's small, just like your child. This takes away a lot of the intimidation factor that can come along with the actual toilet. Plus, it is safer and easier for your child to get onto a small potty independently. Kids tend to be more drawn to things that are their size, not to mention some of the snazzy colors, designs, and features that are available in potties today.

- Posture. A floor potty gives your child great stability and foot support because it's on the ground, almost always putting them in a natural squat position, which is the ideal position for easily releasing their bladder and bowels.

Tips When Choosing a Floor Potty

- **A white floor potty more closely resembles the large toilet and is less easily confused as a toy,** making it a better choice for many families. That said, if your child is super into racecars and has been resistant to potty training, get that race car potty if it entices them to try again!

- **Make sure the potty is easy to clean** without nooks and crannies for pee to get stuck in. A removable bowl for easy cleanup is ideal.

- **Choose something with a good splash guard.** When kids (both boys AND girls!) start peeing in the potty, the spray factor is real. A higher splash guard will save your floors and your sanity.

- **Opt for something budget friendly.** You don't need to purchase expensive potties when it's not something your child will be using long term. Instead, choose a budget-friendly option and get more than one so you have one for each level of the house or one for home and one for the car.

- **If you have a child with a history of constipation, choose a potty with more foot support to help avoid poop problems.** You can learn more about poop issues in my online course, *How to Get Your Child to Poop on the Potty: The Advanced Guide.*

- **If your child needs extra motivation or engagement, choose a potty with added bells and whistles like music or flushing sounds.** If you would rather avoid buttons and noises, you can always let them decorate a normal floor potty with stickers or markers to personalize it.

Pros of Going Straight to the Toilet

- **Easy clean-up.** When your child uses the toilet, the pee and poop (usually) goes straight in, ready to be flushed away. There's no added clean up like you have with a floor potty.

- **Association.** The fact that the toilet is in the bathroom and stays in the bathroom can help kids who are struggling with connecting their bodily functions with the bathroom environment. It makes it easier to maintain the mindset that the toilet is the only place we pee and poop. Sometimes, a floor potty unintentionally turns into a TV watching spot or a snack eating seat, which can lead to confusion about its true purpose.

- **Transition.** By starting off with the toilet, you avoid the possibility of having to transition your child away from the floor potty later on. Not often, but sometimes, kids will become dependent on the floor potty making toilet use much more challenging for them. This can also limit their ability to use the potty in places other than the home. There will be toilet access the majority of places you go, and almost never small potty access unless you bring your own. So, getting that early exposure to the toilet is beneficial for potty use at home, school, restaurants, stores, airports, and more. It's the best option to reach that end goal we're all after: potty independence in any environment.

So, if you are starting potty training from scratch, using both a small floor potty plus exposure to a regular toilet is ideal. Using the small floor potty sets your child up for more successes during those first few days without diapers and while pottying on the go, but using the toilet is going to help them be more comfortable using the potty places other than at home.

There are some cases where it is recommended to skip the small floor potty and use the toilet right off the bat. If your child already has experience with and is comfortable with the toilet, perhaps from school or daycare, or if they are already too big for a floor potty from a size standpoint – then you would be okay to forgo the floor potty and go for the toilet right away. Additionally, if your child has a developmental delay like autism, which can sometimes make transitions or changes more difficult, it is best to start right away with the toilet to avoid the additional transition later on.

Using a Seat Insert on a Toilet

When you decide to incorporate the regular toilet into your child's potty training, whether it be right away or later on, it will be very important to consider safety, stability, and good potty posture. Using a seat insert or seat reducer on top of the toilet is always a good idea for our little potty learners. Here are various types to consider:

- Simple seat with a step stool for foot support. Remember, we never want your child's feet dangling while they're on the toilet. Handles are also a nice feature to give your child something to hold for added stability.
- Small toilet insert with a built-in ladder attachment. Some come with a padded seat ring and an extra step to help your child get into that natural squat, or "prime poop position."
- A child-sized seat that comes attached to an adult seat, which is a more permanent and discreet option. This is particularly great for bathrooms that are used by guests. The toddler seat is built right into the regular toilet seat and can be pulled down whenever your child needs to use the potty. Just remember that your child will still need foot support for this one.

If you aren't quite sure how to decide, get your child involved in the selection process. Bring up pictures of a few options that you're okay with and then let them pick which one they like best to give them a sense of ownership and control. You can find my favorite potty seat options in my Amazon Storefront.

At the end of the day, if your child is using the floor potty, the toilet, or some combination of both, it doesn't matter, because each one is a success!

The Prime Poop Position
- Knees above hips
- Feet flat and fully supported
- Back straight
- Slight forward lean

CHOOSING UNDERWEAR

When it's time to start potty training, skip the temptation to use disposable training pants, more commonly known by their brand name, Pull Ups. To your child, Pull Ups are no different than a diaper that's pulled up and down. They are so absorbent that it's really hard to feel an accident, and therefore, they can easily become a crutch that your child chooses to use instead of using the potty. So, once you're ready to switch over from diapers, plan on transitioning your child straight into underwear, perhaps with the exception of overnight which we will start to address at the end of the chapter.

Selecting your child's first underwear, much like selecting their potty, is a very personal choice. For all children, comfort is obviously a top priority. We don't want your child to protest wearing underwear because they aren't comfortable. But, comfort feels different to different kids. Think about any sensory sensitivities your child might have when it comes to clothing. Tags, seams, or tight fitting elastics could all potentially bother a child who is new to the world of underwear. To help your child feel more excited about the transition, take them shopping and select some they are drawn to. Remember, the more we offer choices during this process, the more in control your child will feel and the less likely you are to encounter power struggles.

Also, opting for a boxer short or boxer brief style underwear for boys or a boy short style for girls will fit less like a diaper and help increase their awareness of their body's urges. Generally, lightweight breathable fabrics are ideal and sizing up from what your child would normally wear makes accidents less easily contained and therefore more uncomfortable. If your child doesn't like the way accidents feel in their new underwear, that will be a deterrent to do it again. Having them fit more loosely will also make it easier for your child to pull them up and down without assistance. You can find my current favorite underwear choices in my Amazon storefront.

A Note On Potty Training Underwear

Potty training underwear, which is essentially regular underwear with a thicker absorbent lining in the crotch area can be tempting to buy. However, it is only recommend to use these in certain situations because the absorbency does not help them raise as much awareness when an accident occurs, which may hinder the learning process and send mixed signals.

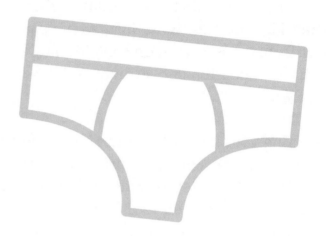

It *is* okay to use training underwear if you are ever tempted to use a Pull Up or diaper out of fear of an accident or for an added convenience factor. Like on a longer car ride, if your commute involves public transportation, if your child is having a hard time mastering dry naps, or if your child's school or daycare isn't quite ready for the switch to regular underwear. So, while they aren't necessary, it doesn't hurt to have a pack on hand for those just-in-case moments.

CONSIDER NIGHTTIME POTTY TRAINING

Knowing what to do for naps and nighttime can be one of the most intimidating things to think about when it comes to potty training. For now, there is a very helpful way to determine if your child is ready to sleep without diapers, and many kids are ready for nighttime potty training before we realize it - even if they are still sleeping in a crib! If you can do both daytime and nighttime training all at once, it will make the entire process shorter, more efficient and show consistency from the beginning. This sends a very clear message to your child that all pee and poop belong in the potty from now on without exceptions.

This said, I encourage you to at least attempt nighttime potty training instead of just waiting for them to wake up dry on their own one day - which could be weeks, months, or YEARS down the road - because research tells us that starting nighttime toilet training earlier results in the attainment of nighttime continence and a lower rate of enuresis, aka involuntary urination, by more than HALF! A 2011 study* of 235 children showed that those who started nighttime potty training before 30 months had an enuresis rate of only 14.3%, whereas those who started after 30 months had a rate of 33.3%. This study proves there are definitely pros to removing those nighttime diapers as soon as possible!

*Yang, S.S.-D., Zhao, L.-L. and Chang, S.-J. (2011), Early initiation of toilet training for urine was associated with early urinary continence and does not appear to be associated with bladder dysfunction†‡. Neurourol. Urodyn., 30: 1253-1257. https://doi.org/10.1002/nau.20982

To help predict how your nighttime potty training journey might look if you decide to embark on it, over the course of about a week (or a minimum of four days), do some nighttime diaper checks. This looks like feeling your child's diaper before you go to bed at night yourself, and then again about 20 to 30 minutes before they wake up in the morning and see how wet it is, if at all. A lot of times, kids are actually holding it all night and then peeing in their diaper upon waking, giving the false impression that they have been wetting themselves all night long. You might find yourself pleasantly surprised!

If your child is saturated for more than half of the checks over the course of a week, then you can either wait and attempt nighttime potty training after they've gotten a good grasp on their daytime potty use for up to six months or you can implement some more in depth training methods which are outlined in Chapter 7, as well as my online course, *Potty Training for Nighttime*. If, on the other hand, they were dry for more than half of these checks, you're good to go with pulling the plug on both nap and nighttime diapers from the very start without having to follow any special tactics! I've included a tracking chart at the end of this chapter for you to record your results.

If your child is a very light sleeper and you can't do this exercise without waking them up and disturbing their sleep, then you can skip it. Instead, try to make a note of how soon they pee again after you change them out of their nighttime diaper. If it's fairly soon, they probably went at some point during sleep. If an hour or more passes, chances are they peed in their diaper when they first woke up!

PREPARING YOUR HOME FOR POTTY TRAINING

It's finally time to prep your house for this undertaking! It's no secret that potty training is a messy business, but there are steps you can take to keep your stress over that mess at bay. Accidents are going to be part of the learning process, so here are a few things to do before the big day:

Roll up area rugs, and if you have carpet in your house, consider picking up a pack of disposable puppy pee pads to line the floor. If there's an accident, you can just toss out the pad that was affected and replace it with a new one. You can also use these to protect couches, high chairs, and strollers. Do not use them in the car seat since they aren't designed for that purpose and can compromise the car seat's safety. Alternatively, you can purchase manufacturer-specific waterproof car seat liners for those travel worries as long as they have been crash tested.

Protect your mattresses. Waterproof mattress covers are a must-have during potty training. They can be disposable or reusable, cover the entire mattress or just lay on top. While you certainly need one for your child's bed, it is good to grab one for yours as well if your kid ever snuggles or sleeps with you there. It's even a good idea to layer mattress pads and sheets for more efficient bedding changes when there is an accident. It may be tempting to go for the cheapest option available, especially considering the work it'll be doing, but buyer beware: many of the cheaper mattress covers can contain harmful chemicals or toxins. Avoid those that contain PVC, which is a known human carcinogen, and/or phthalates which can also be very dangerous to young kids and give off strong odors. Try to opt for products with natural or organic materials instead. If the material it's made from isn't listed, that is a red flag to steer clear.

Prepare a cleaning caddy with paper towels, your favorite cleaning spray, small trash bags, and stain remover. If you're sensitive to mess and smells, you can throw in a mask and gloves too.

Themed decor and an activity basket for the bathroom and an activity basket for the bathroom to add a fun factor. Both you and your child will be spending quite a bit of time in the bathroom in the coming days, so adding some decorations, be it for the next upcoming holiday, a particular interest your child has, or a random mix of things can make it more enjoyable. You may be able to use something you already have, such as a lava or bubble lamp, an artificial fish tank, or a seek and find poster to put at eye level across from the potty. Put together a small potty basket with some fun new activities your child can do during potty time. Fidget toys, an old calculator, bubbles, sticker books, or even kitchen tools that they might not normally play with are all great options to include. Get creative and have fun with this!

Set up a nighttime potty station with a towel or pee pad, a small floor potty, a night light, toilet paper, clean clothes, and extra sheets. Even if you choose not to actively pursue nighttime potty training from the start, your child might still request the potty during nap or nighttime. This creates a quick and convenient spot to use the potty and get right back to sleep.

Hopefully after taking time to go through these preparations, you'll feel confident and prepared. It's now time to say goodbye to those diapers!

Nighttime Diaper Check Results

Feel your child's diaper 20 minutes before they normally would wake up for the course of 3 to 5 days before you start potty training and document if they are dry/damp/fully saturated below. Check the appropriate box.

Day	Dry	Damp	Saturated
1			
2			
3			
4			
5			

Shopping List

Cut along the line and take this page with you to the store or have it handy while you browse my Amazon Storefront!

 FLOOR POTTY

2ND FLOOR POTTY (OPTIONAL)

 UNDERWEAR (12 - 15 PAIRS)

 FLUSHABLE WIPES

 STICKERS &/OR REWARDS

NEW POTTY TIME ACTIVITY

 INSERT FOR TOILET

MATTRESS PROTECTION

 Towels
PUPPY PADS FOR FLOORS/FURNITRUE

NEW BATHROOM DECOR (OPTIONAL)

chapter five

saying goodbye to diapers

No matter how long you decide to spend on the prep work we covered in the first few chapters, it is always helpful to have one designated day to officially say goodbye to diapers and hello to the potty. Having a clear cut day to swear off diapers makes the potty training process more efficient and keeps the expectation that we are trying to put all pee and poop in the potty clear for your child.

I want YOU to feel prepared as you embark on this new journey, so be extra sure that your count down and start date make sense with everything else you have going on. The process might test your willpower to keep going at times, so make sure you've done everything in your power before you begin to help ensure your success the first time around. You are strong and capable and I believe in you.

You've got this!

Action Item!

A note for parents with children who have other caregivers helping with potty training: I've included a Progress Chart at the end of this chapter which will help you document specific things about your child's potty habits and usage to help keep everyone on the same page when that care is transferred over to someone else. Be sure you have this handy on Day One to jot down your notes and observations.

An Ideal First Day Without Diapers

We've already spoken about planning some fun activities to do with your child while you're hanging out at home the first day or two. This could be watching movies, doing arts and crafts, cooking, sensory bins, obstacle courses, or games and puzzles! This will keep everyone's morale up and keep them engaged with you so you can be more closely watching for their signals and cues to use the potty. I like to say, if you are working hard to make your child happy, they're more likely to work hard and make you happy by using the potty correctly. It ends up being a win-win for everyone!

For potty time specifically, have a little basket with a small potty, wipes, books, sensory toys, bubbles, and other fun potty-designated activities you can bring with you around the house to optimize the chance of success.

TAKING OFF THAT LAST DIAPER

When you first wake up in the morning, you should remove your child's pajamas and overnight diaper. With a ceremonial goodbye, throw that final diaper away into the trashcan or diaper pail together with a little song or dance. Use positive energy to encourage your child during this uncertain time!

Some kids are quite attached to their diapers. They can be like a security blanket in a lot of ways. It's been a constant for them since birth, so just throwing them away may not feel very good. If you feel like your child might lean that way, consider having them gift wrap their remaining diapers to give to the mailman to bring to another baby or toddler that needs them more. The baby or toddler can be real or imaginary, but the point of the exercise is to transfer any negative feelings of having to get rid of their beloved diapers into positive feelings of being a helper and a giver.

Some parents have also had luck leaving the leftover diapers out for the "potty fairy". While your child sleeps, replace their diapers with their new undies or a special gift. Most kids won't question their diapers going away then!

Whichever of these options you decide best aligns with your child's personality, it helps them to close the chapter of diapers and move forward to what we've all been waiting for - using the potty successfully!

EMBRACE BOTTOMLESS TIME

Once the diapers are off, your child should have nothing on their lower half for the first day as well as a portion of the second day. This means no diaper, underwear, or pants. Being bottomless accelerates their learning by allowing them to be more aware of what's happening with their body. Up until this point, they've had a trusty diaper to wick away any moisture from peeing or contain their poop without much thought or consequence. By removing their bottoms completely, when the pee and poop start to come, they see and feel that there's nothing left to contain their pee and poop anymore. It has a little shock factor to it, but in a good way. They will begin connecting the urges in their bodies to needing to use the bathroom, and (hopefully) begin to take action all on their own.

Having bottomless time helps your child be more aware, but it helps you too. A large part of these first couple diaper-free days are going to be learning opportunities for you. You'll learn your child's potty habits and routines so you can set them up for as many successes as possible. You've already got activities lined up to do alongside your child for today, so it should be pretty obvious when the pee and/or poop first start coming out so you can try to catch some in the potty. This is a lot easier than when they're wearing underwear and it may take you several minutes to notice that they've peed.

I know this seems pretty daunting, but trust me, the initial mess and hard work will pay off! This leads me into my next tip...

KEEP A POTTY NEARBY

Keeping a small toilet nearby is so important on Day One so that your child has as many successes as possible when just starting out. When that pee or poop starts to come, you most likely aren't going to have much of a warning. But if you have a small floor potty within arms' reach, you can turn potential accidents into successes, making for the BEST learning opportunities.

If pee starts to come, say, "Oh look! You're peeing! Let's get to the potty!" Bring the potty over to them and gently sit them down on it. Try to avoid taking them away from their activity to the toilet, opting for bringing the potty to them, so they don't feel like they're missing out on the activity because of potty training which can lead to frustration and resistance. Even if you catch just a couple drops, celebrate that win!

Try to stay calm when they begin to pee so you don't accidentally startle your child. If they are resistant to sitting down when you bring the potty over to them, don't physically force it. Instead, try to hold the bowl of the potty close by to catch some of the pee if possible. Even just seeing the pee go into the potty and that nothing bad or scary happens can be helpful. Of course, you can't get them all every time, and that's fine too. The more practice they get with getting pee or poop into the potty, the faster they'll learn! We'll cover exactly how to handle accidents in Chapter 7.

After the potty success, depending on how your child is feeling, you can have them walk with you to the bathroom to empty the contents of the potty into the regular toilet, flush, and wash their hands. However, keep in mind that there are a lot of steps involved with potty use and you don't want this first day to become all consumed with potty business, otherwise they could quickly lose interest or become resentful. Sometimes it's just as well to wipe them and let them go back to whatever they were doing. You can gauge that when you're in the moment based on your child's mood.

TO PROMPT, OR NOT TO PROMPT?

When you first say goodbye to diapers, you might be tempted to set a timer and take your child to sit on the potty every 20 or 30 minutes or constantly ask them if they need to pee. While this tactic will get pee in the potty most of the time, the end goal of potty training isn't to solely prevent accidents, it's also to encourage your child to learn how to listen to their body and take themselves to the potty when they need to go. With constant prompting, you run the risk of your child never learning their own body's signals and urges that tell them when to go potty.

To pass urine easily, the bladder muscle is supposed to contract while the pelvic floor muscles relax. This doesn't happen as easily or naturally if there's no urge within the body to go. Your child might be able to squeeze out a little bit of pee, but that's only because the bladder is contracting more aggressively to make it happen. Also, if the bladder is always being emptied before it's reached its full capacity, it will start to "think" it's full when it's actually not. Then you just end up feeling like you have to pee a lot more frequently, and when you do go, it's not how your body is intended to work, creating a vicious cycle.

Mindset shift!

The goal of potty training is not to prevent as many accidents as possible, it is to help your child learn how to listen to their body and take themselves to the potty when they need to go!

So in general, try to avoid using the potty at set times or doing just-in-case pees. Don't get me wrong - there are times when it is okay to make a routine out of using the potty, such as upon waking, before sleep (either nap or nighttime), and whenever you can tell your child physically needs to go. You can also have your child use the potty before leaving the house or before a super stimulating activity like attending a birthday party or playing on the playground until they are really in a solid routine of using the potty reliably on their own. We just don't want to create any negative long-term habits that can carry with them into adolescence. Children with certain disabilities may also do better with being on a potty schedule based on the times that they naturally tend to need to go.

Prompting your child too often or using timed potty visits has some other risks as well. First, your child might simply get frustrated about being made to sit on the potty so often, especially when they don't even need to go, creating resistance, pushback, and power struggles. Also, your child might become so dependent on your prompts that they won't realize that they can go potty without being told to do so first. Their use of the potty becomes your responsibility instead of their own.

Some kids need to pee every few minutes, but others only need to pee every few hours. Both fall in the "normal" range. When you first start potty training, you won't necessarily know where in that range your child falls. This is where you'll be learning about your child's potty habits those first few days. Try to jot down some notes about how often your child seems to need to go, or if there are certain times of day that they are more likely to go in the Progress Chart at the end of the chapter. This way, you can be on the lookout for any physical cues or signals that they need to go potty so you can try to help them learn those signs for themselves, while also setting them up for successful visits to the potty.

IDENTIFYING & INTERPRETING POTTY LANGUAGE

Most children give a signal when they first feel the urge to pee or poop, but they might not recognize what their body is telling them at first, so it's our job to help them along! The signals or, "potty language" as I like to call it, look like a change in behavior or emotions that can be super obvious, very subtle, or anywhere in between. Since you're the expert on your child, you'll likely pick up on this fairly quickly. Being bottomless should make these signs even more apparent.

Potty Language might look like:

- crossing legs
- grabbing or playing with genitals or bottom
- walking on tiptoes
- squatting
- not being able to stand still (aka the "potty dance")
- spike in energy level
- becoming clingy or irritable
- attempting to hide
- for poops, they may stand completely still, stare off into space, grab onto furniture, and/or get red in the face

If you start noticing any of these things from your kiddo, it's time to prompt a visit to the potty. To take the learning one step further so they can eventually self-initiate, help them recognize that their body is sending them these potty signals! Say, "I can see you're crossing your legs. That's your body's way of telling you it needs to go potty. Let's go sit!"

With practice, you'll be able to put the ball into their court by doing these body check-ins. Have them focus on you for a second and ask, "Do you think your body is trying to tell you something right now?" That can help them reach into their interoception – or their ability to understand what's going on inside their body. Interoception is a sense, just like taste, touch, or smell, that tells us when we are hungry, cold, itchy, in pain, or when we need to use the bathroom! This last part isn't something they've had to pay much attention to before because they've always had their diapers, so there is definitely a learning curve at first. Do your best to bring your patience and they should pick up on it fairly quickly.

HANDLING SUCCESSES

A potty success includes ANY pee or poop getting into the potty. This could look like:

- Your child starting to pee or poop while not on the potty, but then getting some into the potty either from your redirection or them realizing and going themselves
- Your child using the potty when prompted by you
- Them sitting on the potty and going themselves

Obviously the last one is the main goal, so you want to be sure you respond to your child accordingly. Start off with general verbal praise. Be specific and say things to trigger their intrinsic, or internal, motivation. For example, "Great job putting your pee in the potty! You should be so proud!" Combine that with some physical affection – a hug, a fist bump, or a high five – and you're really in business! Most kids love being acknowledged by their parents or caregivers for an accomplishment, so this can be super motivating for them to use the potty again and again.

WHAT ABOUT REWARDS?

There is a lot of conflicting information out there about whether using rewards is good or bad. According to a paper written by parenting expert Alan Kazdin in 2017, rewards help children to get "repeated practice" of a non-preferred activity, i.e. an activity they don't love doing, such as toileting, which then turns into a habit.

Some people argue that rewards will decrease a child's intrinsic motivation to use the toilet. But a 2001 article by Cameron, Banko, and Pierce used decades of research and found that rewards only diminish intrinsic motivation if:

- rewards are used for an activity that the child is already highly interested in (which is unlikely to be true for potty training)
- the reward is expected, like a bribe
- it is not clearly related to performance (meaning it doesn't happen immediately or consistently after successfully using the toilet)

Parenting training programs that use rewards have been found to have significant and long-lasting improvements in child behavior as found by Long, Forehand, Wierson, & Morgan in 1994. Lastly, the use of rewards can actually improve the parent-child relationship as found by Wiggins, Sofronoff, & Sanders in 2009.

In summary

Research suggests that you shouldn't be afraid to use rewards for toilet training!

A few notes about choosing rewards:

1. **Select something that is really desirable for your child, not something they get access to on a regular basis.** This could be something edible, tangible , or experiential. You can find some ideas for each category listed below! They will be more encouraged to use the potty if the prize isn't something they get access to for any other reason. Bonus tip: make the reward more enticing by adding the element of surprise. Wrap each prize and keep them all in a small basket, make a surprise box that they can blindly reach into, or use an advent calendar where they randomly open a door to find a new prize.

2. **Keep the reward exclusive to potty successes.** This means the actual act of peeing or pooping in the potty – not just sitting and trying, not simply asking for a prize, but for actual pee or poop going in the potty. If it starts off as an accident but your child is then able to get some pee or poop into the potty, then that would count as a success and can be rewarded! As we talked about above, you're going to want to give them the reward consistently and immediately after they've finished using the potty to help make the connection between the behavior and the reward itself.

3. **Keep the prizes going for about a week.** Once they have been using the potty consistently for a good five to seven days, the habit should be ingrained enough that you can start cutting back on the rewards. Be wary of stopping rewards cold turkey, unless your child has already lost interest in them. Instead, wean off of them gradually. Start by setting slightly longer-term goals that can be kept track of on a chart or calendar instead of rewarding each individual potty success. You can first try for a great potty day, then a week, then two weeks, and then a month. Each time you increase the goal, increase the value of the reward to match. So instead of an M&M, have a movie night or dessert of their choice after dinner. For a successful potty week, you can let them choose their own toy from the store. For a whole month, you can take them to the aquarium or a special event. Think about what is motivating for your child!

4. **Go simple with a sticker chart.** If all this feels to be a bit much, grab a piece of paper that they get to slap a special sticker on with each potty success. This paper then becomes a great visual representation of all the times they used the potty throughout the day, and it's a super fun thing to celebrate all together as a family each evening.

Reward Ideas

EDIBLE

- M&Ms
- Jelly beans
- Gummy bears
- Goldfish
- Chocolate chips (morsels)
- Yogurt covered raisins
- Cereal pieces
- Mini marshmallows
- Mini ice pops (freeze juice in ice cube molds!)

TANGIBLE

- Stickers
- Small toys (add an element of surprise by wrapping them like tiny gifts!)
- Books
- Party favors
- Hand stamps
- Temporary tattoos
- Charms for charm bracelet
- Pom poms in a jar
- Puzzle pieces

EXPERIENTIAL (AND FREE!)

- Painting fingernails (one nail per potty success)
- Trip to the fire station
- Nature walk
- Watching the garbage truck
- Baking or cooking together
- Trip to the pet store
- Watching airplanes/
- construction vehicles
- Library story time
- Getting to choose daily outfit
- Getting to choose what meal you have for dinner
- Staying up 15 minutes late
- Screen time

GRETA'S big girl
potty chart

DAY 1
DAY 2
DAY 3

Apply the knowledge

This section will help you to prepare for the first few days of potty training so you know what to expect. It should keep you feeling confident and optimistic about the experience!

THIS is our ideal start date and **WE ARE STICKING WITH IT!!**

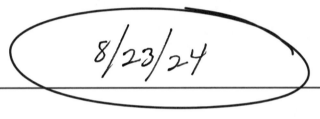

8/23/24

Ideas of potty-time activities:	Here are some potty-exclusive distractions my child can do while they sit on the potty:	
	✓ Books	**Other Ideas:**
	Videos	
	✓ Bubbles	
	✓ Coloring books	
	✓ Sensory toys	
	Play Doh	
	✓ Songs	

Reward ideas:	What incentives/rewards can you use for potty successes? Remember it should be exclusive to the potty and given immediately after the success.
● Edible	Gummy Bears - poops?
● Tangible	Sticker on chart - pee + poop
● Experiential	

Jot down the times that your child goes to the potty and/or any patterns you notice:

Day One	Day Two
• 7:25 Pee, ask to go	7am wake up, pee in pull up
• 9:30 Pee, ask to go, lots of pee	7:15-8:45 lots of farts, poop sits.
• pee pokes in between	9:00 went to potty + peed on floor
• 11:50 ask to pee but no pee	— by potty
• 12:00 a little water + Mac N Chees	9:39 water + 1 cup watermelon
1:15 naps no pee since 9:30 lots of tries	10:44 Peed on the carpet, nothing in the potty
4pm naps wake up, dry pull up, pee in potty right after	several tries
5:15, 25 asked to go poop, sat + nothing (did ask to put on diaper for poop)	11:53 successful pee in potty
• lots of poop trips	1:10 Nap
6:50 big poop in potty	3:30 wake-up, wet pull up sat on potty + she tried to pee
	4:30 Cherries + milk
	5:10 pee in pants, put on potty + nothing in then
	5:30 pee in potty, pulled pant + she made it wants to be worked
	6:08 Poop in potty, she ran over after seven tries on her own
	6:47 pooped pant while eating bite 7:45 bedtime

Potty language:	List any signs your child shows when they need to use the potty:

Potty Progress Chart

On the first few days of potty training, use this chart to make notes about your child's potty habits and preferences. Then, make copies to hand out to your care team to keep things as consistent as possible!

This is how frequently my child pees:	~2hrs if not drinking a lot ~1hr after drink or fruit
At home we prompt a potty visit at these times:	~ 90 minutes
My child poops this many times per day:	1-2 times
My child usually poops at these times each day:	The last two days evening, but could be at any time
My child shows the following potty language when they need to go:	Grabs bottom or grabs front
My child prefers to do these things while on the potty (song, book, activity, etc.):	Song or book
My child has a preference about privacy vs company in the bathroom. It is:	Sometimes she like company + reading Other times privacy. I try + ask her
We are using these rewards at home:	High fives, knuckles stickers on a chart
We typically say this for a potty success:	Good job, your tummy probably feels good.
This is our process and language for handling an accident:	You peed in your pants, pee goes in the potty. Lets get you cleaned up.

chapter six

sitting, standing, & wiping

SHOULD MY BOY STAND OR SIT TO PEE?

A common question I am asked by parents of boys is if they should sit or stand to pee. **My answer is always the same: SIT!** This is because asking your little guy to sit when they poop but stand when they pee adds unnecessary confusion in an already unpredictable time. It's also better from a safety standpoint. When your son is first starting to learn how to use the potty, he's probably too short to reach the toilet to pee into without standing on something. Standing up on a stepstool while trying to aim properly is a lot for a child to focus on! Sitting is simply safer.

Another aspect to consider is the mess. Potty training is messy as it is, and as a boy mom myself, I can attest to how messy they can be when they stand up to pee (for many years to come I might add). So I'm thinking of you on this one – you don't need the added stress and frustration! Sitting on the potty won't always be mess free, but it does make it much more likely that they'll get the pee in the bowl where it belongs.

Bottom line

Keep things as simple and consistent as possible for your little guy, at least until they are peeing and pooping on the potty consistently before adding in the aspect of standing to pee.

Eventually when they are a potty pro, are tall enough to reach the toilet without a step stool, and are showing an interest in standing, you can teach them. This is a place for dad or another trusted male role model to step in. Using public bathrooms where urinals are available or standing to pee outside can be good places to start introducing this skill. There are toilet targets you can purchase to help them make it into the bowl, but a lot of people simply toss a couple cheerios into the toilet for them to aim at!

Keep in mind that there is no harm in a boy sitting to pee – in fact, a lot of urologists and pelvic floor specialists claim it is a better physical position to fully void the bladder. So he can sit as long as he, or you, wants to. It's all about doing what your family feels most comfortable with.

WIPING

I know you're wondering: How long am I going to be wiping bums?!

One thing I know crosses every parent's mind, especially once you've started potty training is: HOW LONG AM I GOING TO BE WIPING BUMS?! I hate to break the bad news – you've probably still got a ways to go. Generally speaking, girls will master wiping faster than boys because their fine motor skills develop more quickly than boys and they wipe for both pee and poop, so they have a lot more opportunities to practice.
Here are some tips to help encourage this final step of potty independence:

Keep your expectations low. The harsh reality is, many toddlers and preschoolers aren't even physically proportioned to be able to wipe effectively until they are closer to 4 years old or older. Their little arms aren't quite long enough to reach around for that proper front to back wiping technique which is important for proper hygiene. All you can do initially is practice. They are still going to need you to go behind them with quality checks for a while to ensure they are getting themselves nice and clean.

Practice wiping in the bathtub. Spread some suds or conditioner on their bottom and let them wipe with a washcloth. This is a great opportunity to teach and practice the front to back wiping motion.

Teach the WFR (wipe, fold, repeat) by spreading some peanut butter on a plastic doll's bottom, give them a wipe and have them practice wiping, folding, wiping, folding, etc. until nothing else comes off on the wipe and the baby doll is clean. If you don't want to use peanut butter, you can also do washable markers!

A note about wipes: Using flushable or wet wipes is generally recommended when your child is learning to wipe after a poop for ease of use and better hygiene. They simply clean better than dry toilet paper with less effort and less waste. That said, even if a wipe is labeled "flushable", it is not. Every plumber or public works professional I've ever spoken to says to NOT flush wipes, no matter what. They can cause thousands of dollars in damage to your plumbing. So, just toss them into the trash instead.

If the thought of having poopy wipes in your trashcan grosses you out – and I can't really blame you there – consider toilet paper sprays. These products turn regular toilet paper into a wet wipe, and then they are completely safe to flush. My favorite option is in my Amazon Storefront.

Apply the knowledge

As always, we want to think about the best ways YOUR child can learn these new skills. Use this space to make some notes and jot down ideas.

Based on your family's preferences, will your son sit or stand to pee?

⬤ Sit   ⬤ Stand

Who is a trusted male role model that can help him learn when the time is right?

_____

What struggles might your child have with wiping?

List some toys and supplies you have on hand to help teach wiping:

chapter seven

accidents, naptime, & nighttime

HANDLING ACCIDENTS

Along with successes, there will likely be a fair share of accidents during the first couple of days. They are simply bound to happen. Dealing with potty accidents is certainly one of the most frustrating parts of the whole potty training process, and it's probably one of the main reasons parents do not look forward to this stage. But, accidents are a completely normal part of the process, and they actually help your child to learn more quickly.

Every child makes mistakes when learning a new skill. Every time we make a mistake, our brain generates new pathways to prevent us from making that same mistake again. Remind yourself of this as you're going through it. Be patient, calm, and try to avoid getting frustrated. Many people tend to keep track of the number of accidents during potty training as a way to gauge progress, but really you should only be keeping track of the successes.

In the beginning, accidents are due to the fact that your child doesn't possess the muscle control or awareness to make it to the potty in time yet. Retraining their muscles away from the automatic release into the diaper to holding it until they can make it to the potty will take time to figure out. Whenever your child says they need to use the potty, do your best to take them right away as the time between your child realizing they need to go and the pee/poop actually coming out is probably less than a few seconds.

Even once your child starts using the potty, accidents can still happen, and this is normal. Most of the time accidents come as a result of being distracted. If your child is engrossed in an activity, like playing outside for example, two things tend to occur: they are less aware of the sensation of needing to go potty until it starts happening or they hold it in so they don't have to stop the activity, potentially until it's too late. Accidents are also more likely to occur when your child is sick, very tired, or excited.

Mindset shift!

Accidents are completely normal and should be expected - even welcomed! - during the potty training process. When your child has an accident, it is actually helping them to learn even faster!

Keep your response to an accident minimal and matter-of-fact.

No matter the reason for the accident, there should never be any shaming, scolding, or punishment. At the same time, you don't necessarily want to be too comforting either, because that could actually make your child falsely believe that accidents are acceptable. A minimal, matter-of-fact reaction works best. If you aren't able to catch any pee/poop in the potty once the accident starts, quickly acknowledge the situation by saying, "Oops, you peed on the floor. Remember, pee only goes in the potty now. Let's try harder to get there next time."

After an accident, even if you think there is nothing left to come out, sit your child on the potty as they get cleaned up because they may not have fully voided. If they get anything in the potty at that point, treat it as a success!

If you find that accidents are persistent and not improving, it can help to exaggerate the cleanup process. We don't want your child thinking that having an accident is more convenient than using the potty! Be sure your child stops playing until everything is cleaned up, and do a thorough wipe-down or even bathe them before changing their clothes. This shows your child that it is faster to just use the potty initially instead of going in their pants or on the floor. You can also have them participate in the cleanup if you think that would be a deterrent based on your child's personality. If you decide to use this tactic, remember it should not be as a form of punishment, rather as an automatic and consistent result to the behavior. To further drive this home, when your child does use the potty, you can comment on how fast it was. "Great job putting your pee in the potty. See how fast that was? Now you can get right back to playing!"

Occasionally, some children will have small dribbles in their underwear before making it to the potty, not even enough to penetrate through to make their pants wet. This is normal and shouldn't be considered an accident. It is your child's way of testing the limits to see how long they can go before stopping and getting to the potty. Remind them to stop and go as soon as they feel the need. As their muscle control improves, the behavior should diminish. If it persists for longer than a week or two, it could be a sign of an out-of-sync pelvic floor or low muscle tone that needs improving. You can always reach out to a medical professional like a pediatric physical therapist for advice.

GO DIAPERLESS FOR NAPTIME

I know it may seem scary, but your child is no longer going to be in diapers or Pull Ups for naptime starting on Day One of potty training.

This part might be a little scary and feel like it goes against everything you thought you knew about potty training, but I need you to trust me. Starting from day one, your child is no longer going to wear diapers or Pull Ups for naptime. Removing all the daytime diapers sends the clear message that ALL pee and poop goes into the potty. Putting a diaper on midday after you said goodbye to diapers in the morning can lead to confusion and mixed signals. Some children will even withhold their pee and poop until they get access to that naptime diaper, leaving you with no potty successes. We need to trust in their abilities and give them the credit they deserve. Sure, the first couple of days as they are learning and getting adjusted to the new routine might result in wet naps, but most kids are perfectly capable of staying dry for naptime right from the get go.

To help them stay dry throughout naptime, have them use the potty before they get into their bed or crib. For the first three to five days, they should nap bottomless to help with awareness and give them easy access to the potty in a pinch. Try to get them out of bed right as they are waking up, if not a couple minutes before they would normally wake up and use the potty immediately. Within the first couple of days, you will most likely be pleasantly surprised at how far they've come. After those first few dry naps, you can reintroduce clothing for sleep time.

Keep in mind

Your child is capable of way more than you think! They will likely be able to stay dry for naps within the first few days of starting.

TRY TO POTTY TRAIN FOR NIGHTTIME TOO

Most parents opt to get their kiddo in a good place with daytime potty training before deciding to ditch the diapers for nighttime, and I totally understand the desire to preserve everyone's precious sleep! But, for sake of efficiency and consistency, I encourage you to say goodbye to all diapers – day and night – from the very start. Not only does it further reinforce the new expectations that all pee and poop go into the potty, but it also prevents your child from withholding until they get access to their nighttime diaper, especially for pooping, which can be a really hard habit to break.

Mindset shift!

The simple fact is, many children are ready to sleep through the night without diapers well before we might realize it!

Even when your child has a super saturated diaper each morning when you go in to get them out of bed, they could be holding their bladder through the night and releasing as soon as they first wake up in the morning out of habit, comfort, and convenience.

Notes:

We already talked about our nighttime potty prep a few chapters ago, which will help you determine how ready your child is to sleep without diapers and how to guide the nighttime portion of potty training.

I have an entire online course dedicated to nighttime potty training, so I would recommend checking that out if you need more details.

Tips to Facilitate Nighttime Dryness

- **Limit fluids after dinnertime.** Keep your child's fluid intake to around four ounces or less between dinner and bedtime, or about 1.5 to 2 hours before sleep. We don't want to withhold fluids altogether as staying hydrated is important for bladder function and health. If your child is a big drinker and limiting fluids in the evenings is a problem, consider offering liquids throughout the day so they get the most in the morning and a minimal amount by bedtime.

- **Have a nighttime potty station.** Keep a small floor potty on a towel or waterproof pad close to your child's bed or crib to make nighttime potty visits more manageable. Use a nightlight and keep a roll of toilet paper or wipes and a stack of dry clothes and sheets out just in case too. This way, no one is fumbling around in the dark and you don't need to turn the lights on, which would completely stimulate and awaken your child. This helps everyone get back to bed as quickly as possible.

- **Sleep bottomless.** Put your child to bed completely bottomless for the first three to five nights. This will help with urge awareness while sleeping, and it will make it much faster and easier to get your child from bed to potty if they call for help in the night. It also makes for less laundry!

- **Perform a double void:** two potty visits close together to ensure the bladder is as empty as possible before going to bed. Have one potty sit at the beginning of your child's bedtime routine and another within 20 to 30 minutes right before they climb into bed.

- **Do some practice runs.** Remember, kids thrive on routine and predictability, and this whole sleeping without a diaper thing is brand new to them. Taking off their diaper and telling them to use the potty in the night if they need to go probably won't cut it. Instead, create a little game where your kiddo pretends to be asleep in their bed, you tickle their belly and say, "Wake up! You need to go potty," and have them get out of bed and sit on the potty as they would in the night and then crawl back into bed. This will help them get more familiar with what might actually go down in the night when they need to go, and it makes things fun!

- **Move wake up time 15 minutes earlier.** The most likely time that your child, or anyone really, needs to pee is first thing when they wake up in the morning. Until now, your child is used to waking up and releasing in their diaper right away. Try to beat them to it and get them out of bed either just before they would normally wake up or right as they are waking up to try and catch a pee in the potty to start off your day.

Ultimately, this journey is yours, and if you feel like your child isn't ready for nighttime potty training or like you just can't handle it right now for one reason or another, I support that decision. Some options to still prevent confusion and mixed signals while not actively pursuing nighttime dryness are: switch to a cloth option that feels more like your child's daytime underwear. Cloth diapers are a good choice because they aren't quite as absorbent as disposable diapers (which I know can defeat the purpose in some cases), but it allows more learning to take place. Also, you can change from diapers to Pull Ups OR switch the brand you've been using so they look very different from what your child is used to. Refer to all of these things as "nighttime undies" so the word "diaper" is out of the conversation completely. The expectation that we should try hard to get all pee and poop in the potty is still there, but you also have that absorbance in case of accidents for added peace of mind.

Again, this is only skimming the surface of nighttime potty training which can be one of the last pieces of the potty training puzzle to come together. I would highly recommend grabbing my affordable online course, *Potty Training for Nighttime*, to learn more.

Apply the knowledge

Do accidents tend to occur during screen time, meals, or when they're distracted from a parent getting home from work? Write down your observations here so you can help your child read their body's cues, even when their mind is elsewhere.

What nighttime strategies will you apply?	⬤ Earlier wake up	⬤ Practice runs
	⬤ Limiting fluids	⬤ Potty station
	⬤ Double void	
	⬤ Sleep bottomless	

chapter eight

incorporating clothing

WHEN TO ADD CLOTHING

We talked about how having one to two days of being totally bottomless can speed up the learning process, and you'll probably see some great successes with this approach. But before long, it's time to incorporate clothing.

I know it can be tempting to stay in one phase when you feel like you're starting to see progress, but it's important to not stay bottomless for too long. The initial bottomless phase helps your child recognize that there isn't going to be anything there to catch their pee and poop anymore. But ultimately, they are going to need to wear clothes again and you don't want to end up with a child who only knows how to use the potty when they are naked.

Depending on how much practice with using the potty your child has gotten in on the first day, or if you only have a weekend to lay down the foundation of new potty skills, you might decide to introduce clothing as soon as on Day Two of no more diapers. If the first day didn't result in much potty practice, or if you have some more time to spend, you can practice another full day of bottomless time if needed.

Otherwise, reintroducing clothing for the second half of Day Two is typically most effective. When your child wakes up from their nap, or after lunch if your child no longer naps, you can put on some loose fitting pants or shorts – no underwear just yet – and then go about the rest of your day to test the waters. Having one layer instead of two right off the bat will mimic the bottomless feeling better and gradually ease them into wearing clothes again.

Full disclosure:

There most likely will be more accidents when you put bottoms back on! This is totally normal. As with everything, it's going to take some practice for your kiddo to adjust.

Remember, they've spent their entire lives up to this point peeing and pooping in diapers, just letting things flow without even thinking, so when you put clothes back on at first, that automatic muscle memory could kick back in and trigger more accidents. Do your best to remain patient and consistent. Whatever you do, stay the course. Avoid going back to bottomless or the process will just take that much longer.

Instead, apply some of the knowledge you have gained up to this point. Offer reminders to use the potty about as often as they were peeing or pooping the first day or two. Simply say, "Remember, you don't have your diapers anymore! If you feel it, your potty is right here." A reminder is different from a prompt. You won't necessarily be requesting for them to sit on the potty at these times, but you're just keeping the idea fresh in their minds. You'll still be on the lookout for that potty language to help them recognize their body's urges, and it's perfectly okay to take them to use the potty at those times.

After you've put pants or shorts back on, you can help your child practice pulling their pants up and pushing them down to work towards independence with all the steps of potty use. A hand over hand technique works well, as well as incorporating extra practice in fun ways like through pretend fashion shows or dressing and undressing baby dolls. Try to stick with loose, elastic waistbands and steer clear of zippers, buttons, or anything too tight for the first couple of weeks as your child is honing this new skill. Dressing and undressing is a fairly advanced fine motor skill, so don't fret if your child needs help with this portion for a while.

Now, once you have had at least a half a day with your child being in one layer of clothing, you can introduce their cool new underwear! You can make it fun and exciting by wrapping them like a gift or having a "graduation from diapers to undies" ceremony. This is a huge milestone for your child and they should feel proud! Remember to keep the underwear lightweight and loose fitting, and if you can find a cut other than the typical brief style – like a boxer or boy short, that is an added bonus. All of these variables will make the underwear feel less like a diaper, help with body awareness, and make accidents less easily contained, and therefore more noticeable.

If your child starts having multiple, recurring accidents after you bring underwear into the picture, it's okay to stick with one layer instead of two for the first several days. This continues their learning but still allows you to be out in public. That said, let's talk about how to get back out into the real world sans-diaper.

To encourage independence with dressing and undressing, be sure to have clothing on hand that is:

- free of zippers or buttons
- loose fitting
- lightweight

chapter nine

it's time to leave the house

Don't be held hostage by potty training.

One of my many mantras is, "Don't be held hostage by potty training!" It is something that should fit into your existing routine. There are a lot of potty training methods out there that require being at home for a certain period of time, and frankly, with our busy lifestyles today, that's just not realistic. Also, your child is more capable than we give them credit for! They're going to need to learn how to use the potty both in and out of the home. So, after you spend Day One at home saying goodbye to diapers, getting some practice with and exposure to pee and poop going into the potty, go ahead and try getting back out of the house.

I'm not saying take your child to a birthday party at a bounce house or anything, but by Day Two, or after you've introduced that first layer of clothing back into the picture, try going for a walk around the neighborhood or having a picnic in the backyard. Since this outing is the first time your child will have ventured out of the house without the security and comfort of a diaper, you'll want to set them up for success as much as possible. Avoid going somewhere in the car, on public transportation, or super stimulating environments with a lot of distractions. Plan it right after your child has used the potty and stay out of the house for about 30 or 40 minutes. If they're able to make it through dry, offer lots of praise for keeping their clothes dry when you get back. If they have an accident, that's okay too. Staying close to home will make it easier to get back for quick cleanup.

By the third day, or as soon as you feel brave enough, try car outings. Ultimately you are building up to being able to be out and about just like you used to when you had diapers. Also keep in mind that kids are creatures of habit and they like having their regular daily routines. For many children, that means going back to school or a family member's house while their parents return to work after the weekend. That can still totally happen after you've made the switch from diapers to potty!

When you start to go out for longer periods of time, it's helpful to take a travel potty along for the ride. A lot of kids won't feel comfortable using public bathrooms right off the bat – frankly I still don't – or they might not have the control needed to hold it long enough to get to a place that

has bathroom access. When shopping for a travel potty, think about portability (is it easy to take along with you?) and stability (is your child going to be safe while using it?). My favorites can be found in my Amazon Storefront.

Practice with the travel potty at home before using it out and about so your child's first exposure isn't during a time of duress when they really need to go but they aren't sure about this new contraption they've never seen before! In addition, let your child know you have it and show it to them before leaving the house or once you're in the car so they know it is available for them to use if needed. To ease into public bathrooms, when you get to a new place other than home, point out where the bathrooms are at that place and offer to let them check it out if they're curious. Kids don't always realize there are bathrooms everywhere which can cause them to hold it too long and have an accident.

If your child is having a hard time transitioning to public bathrooms, start off by introducing them to bathrooms in other familiar places besides home, such as family member's or friend's homes, or the bathroom at school. Move to family style or single stall type bathrooms in public places like the library, grocery store, or mall, and then slowly acclimate them to regular multi-stall bathrooms by inviting them in to explore, without putting any pressure on them to actually go. If you go first to demonstrate, it can help them get on board and be willing to try too.

Build Your Potty Training Survival Kit to Boost Your Confidence

I acknowledge that it can be quite daunting to venture back out of the house without diapers those first couple of times. Give yourself some added confidence by converting your current diaper bag into a Potty Training Survival Kit. It doesn't need to be anything fancy!

How to build the ideal Potty Training Survival Kit:

- Swap out diapers for extra underwear and a couple changes of clothes
- Add the travel potty
- Old burp cloths or microfiber towels work great to soak up accidents
- A wet bag, small plastic bags, or diaper disposal bags can hold wet or soiled clothing and keep it separate from your dry stuff until you get home
- Bring along potty rewards for celebrating successes on the go to remain consistent
- Hand sanitizer (I like to call it "special soap"!) or sanitizing wipes are a great option to avoid loud hand dryers in public bathrooms
- Sticky notes can cover up the automatic flush sensor which can lead to a traumatizing bathroom experience if it goes off while your child is on the potty!
- Don't forget a spare shirt for yourself. If your child has an accident and you need to quickly scoop them up and head to the bathroom, some of that pee or poop could end up on you too.

Murphy's Law definitely applies to potty training. If you have it, you won't need it. If you don't have it, you'll definitely need it! Being prepared with all the supplies you could possibly need while you're out will make things go a lot more smoothly.

Apply the knowledge

Let's plan your first two outings with your child. Where are some low key places you can you go for 30-45 minutes near your house to help build potty training confidence outside of the home?

Outing 1:

Outing 2:

Think about what you or your child might not enjoy about public restrooms. What are some things you can do to prevent an unpleasant experience?

Potty Training Survival Kit Checklist

Make sure you have each of these items for a kit full of confidence as you leave the house the first few times post potty training!

- Extra underwear

- Two full changes of clothes

- Socks and shoes

- Your travel potty

- Old burp cloths/absorbent towels

- Wet bags/diaper disposal bags/plastic bags

- Potty rewards

- Hand sanitizer

- Sticky Notes

- A spare shirt for you

chapter ten

using the potty with others

IN ADDITION TO USING THE POTTY IN OTHER PLACES, YOUR CHILD IS PROBABLY ALSO GOING TO NEED TO LEARN HOW TO USE THE POTTY WITH OTHER CAREGIVERS.

Whether they go to daycare or preschool, a family member or nanny cares for them during the day, or even if you just have an occasional babysitter, practicing this early can prevent any real preferences from developing. So right from the start, whenever possible, have other caregivers involved.

If your child is hesitant, start off with the other caregiver being just outside the bathroom door, then in the bathroom at the same time as the preferred caregiver, and then eventually with the preferred caregiver just outside the door. Be sure to offer extra praise and comfort for any strides in this area so your child fully understands that everything is okay and they are doing the right thing! It is also helpful to work with your child more on becoming totally independent with their potty use so they don't need assistance from anyone else during the process. That way they can just take themselves to the potty when they need to go.

BACK TO SCHOOL

After your initial two to three days, it's probably time to return to daycare or preschool if your child attends. As I mentioned earlier, you should always speak to your child's caregivers before starting potty training. This ensures that everyone can be on the same page once the diapers are gone and allows you to learn of any special policies or requirements the school or daycare center might have so those things can be taken into account during the training process.

Take a copy or two of your completed Progress Chart to hand out to the classroom teachers so they have a loose plan to refer back to throughout the day. Having something formal written down will help your child's caregiver provide the best continuity of care. It's not a great idea to have them think on the fly with the potential to make a decision that could alter your hard-earned progress!

Caregivers should be made aware of things like:

- What you call the potty. It helps if that vocabulary is the same in all environments. If you call it "potty" at home, but the teacher refers to it as the "restroom" it could lead to confusion.

- Your child's potty language

- How often they use the bathroom

- How you handle accidents and any specific language you use or prefer to avoid

- How sleep situations are handled (Pull Ups, cloth diapers, regular underwear, etc.)

- How you respond to successes. Keep in mind that teachers might not be able to offer a reward for potty successes in a school setting.

- Poop schedule

- Potty preferences (certain book or video, privacy vs. someone in the room, likes to flush vs. scared to flush, etc.)

You will also need to provide the caregiver with any necessary supplies, such as:

- Your child's potty or seat insert (if allowed, many state regulations do not allow this for hygiene reasons)

- Any rewards or stickers being used (again, if allowed)

- A "potty buddy," meaning a familiar toy from home that your child can take to the bathroom with them when they need to go for added comfort and confidence

- A family photo – used in similar fashion to the potty buddy

You can also ask if the teachers are willing to, at least loosely, keep track of the times your child uses the bathroom or has accidents so observations regarding their potty schedule can still be made along with any differences between being at home versus being with them. There is still going to be a lot of learning and development of skills taking place over the next few weeks, so things might need adjusting to accommodate any changes.

The first day your child returns to school after potty training, there are a couple of things you can do to help them feel more comfortable using the bathroom in that new environment. First, at drop off, do a little tour of the bathroom your child will be using there. If your child has some experience with it already, have them lead. See if they can show you things like the toilet, the sink, and how to turn on the light. Really play up how awesome it all seems with phrases like, "Whoa I wish we had foamy soap like that! So cool!" or "This little toilet is so cute! It's exactly your size! Can you show me how you sit on it?" If they are able to sit and test out the potty with

you still there, that's an added bonus to help them feel more confident when you've left.

The next thing you can do is have a little meeting with you, your child, and your child's teacher to clarify that it's okay for them to ask for help if they need to use the potty while you're away. Get down to your child's eye level and say, "If you need to go potty at school today, just ask Mrs. X and she will help you. Right, Mrs. X?" Have the teacher verbally affirm that she is there and happy to help. Sometimes kids can be very shy about asking another grown up about this at first, so if they are certain they can, they'll feel much safer and reassured.

Please remember that as your child transitions back to school that you might see more accidents at first. This is very normal, so please don't get discouraged by this. Most of the time, with consistency, your child's success will quickly fall back into place. If you find that your child's accidents aren't improving at school, dive into some of the troubleshooting topics we will cover in the next chapter.

Apply the knowledge

My child will return to school for the first time without diapers on

DATE: _____

Be sure to plan extra time this day to walk your child through pottying at school and chat with their teacher about how the process is going.

What items might you need to bring with you on this first day?

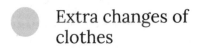 Extra changes of clothes

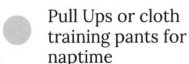 Pull Ups or cloth training pants for naptime

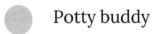 Potty buddy

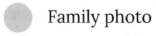 Family photo

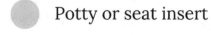 Potty or seat insert

 Rewards

 Progress chart

---

To Do List:

- Pack extra supplies.

- Make copies of Progress Chart.

- Meet with the teacher (with and without your child).

- Tour the bathroom with your child.

- Point out cool things about the bathroom they'll be using.

BONUS: *Let your child overhear you bragging about their new potty skills to their teacher!*

correcting common challenges

POTTY FEAR

Some parents encounter what seems to be their child having a genuine fear of the potty or toilet or a fear of releasing their pee or poop without the comfort of their diapers. It's important to realize that no matter how far-fetched these fears seem to us, to your child, they are their reality. If your child screams, cries, or clings to you when you try to put them on the potty, that's a good sign that the issue is more deeply rooted than just a resistance to change.

While I know it's frustrating and you seem like you can't make any progress with potty training if your child won't even come into the bathroom, have some faith. There are ways to help your child come around. And believe it or not, avoidance of the issue (and this applies to any fear or anxiety!), can actually intensify that fear and make it last longer. But if you gently push them a little harder every few days or weeks, they will eventually get there.

There are multiple steps involved when it comes to potty training, so sometimes you can keep the learning moving in the right direction by simply removing the steps that frighten your child. If your child gets upset about sitting on the toilet, work on washing hands and pulling pants up and down. Gradually encourage them to get closer to the toilet each time you're in the bathroom, until they can comfortably rest their hand on the lid. Then move towards them sitting on your lap while you sit on the toilet, then they can sit on the toilet fully clothed with the lid down, and so on. Gently push them a little outside their comfort zone each time or every few days.

Keep in mind
If your child is so fearful that it results in unhealthy habits such as withholding until the point of discomfort, or physically harming themselves in order to not sit on the potty, it could be an indicator that they are not yet emotionally ready for potty training.

Keep in mind that there are a lot of sensory things happening with potty use too. Sometimes sensory issues don't pop up until the potty training phase which can catch us off guard. Try to put yourself in your child's shoes to uncover the problem. Here are some examples:

- Does your child not like loud noises? Maybe they are scared of the flush. Try letting them wear noise canceling headphones or assure them that you'll wait to flush when they're out of the room.

- Does your child avoid tags in clothing? Maybe they don't like the feeling of the elastic waistband in their new underwear. Try going up a size so it's not as tight or let them try different options to see what they like best.

- Does your child prefer soft surfaces? They might not like the feeling of the hard toilet seat or the bathroom tile under their feet. Try a padded toilet seat or a fuzzy rug to make them feel more comfortable.

- Finding ways to make the bathroom experience satisfying from a sensory standpoint for your child might just eliminate the fears that they were experiencing!

THE FIRST DAY WENT WELL...BUT DAY TWO & THREE? NOT SO MUCH

I have so many parents that get off to a great start the first couple of days, and then by day three or four, things take an ugly turn. You might encounter a child who was happily using the potty multiple times a day or two ago who now refuses to sit, has constant accidents, and melts down at any suggestion of the potty. This is actually normal.

I've said it a few times already - kids thrive best on predictability and routine. But, over the past couple of days since you've started potty training, their little worlds have been rocked. Some kids start to resist the potty because the first couple of days it was new, fun, and exciting, but then the shine wears off. The reality that this is the new norm sets in, and your child might push back a little to see if they can get back to their original comfort zone of diapers. If this isn't your first attempt at potty training, they might be remembering past experiences that the change wasn't permanent then, so they assume it won't be now either. They might be testing limits to see what it takes for you to cave and say, "Enough of this potty business, here have a diaper."

When this type of resistance presents itself, especially after a couple of "good" days of potty use, it's important to persevere through the struggles so your child can see that this new potty stuff isn't going anywhere. Don't give up when the going gets tough! Ultimately, our kids are looking to us for guidance as well as our response to certain situations and behaviors. If they see that you are committed to your decision and that you have confidence in their abilities, they'll come back around. This doesn't mean that you need to feed into the power struggles and physically force your child to sit on the potty on the days that they are extra resistant. However, you'll want to set them up with all the tools they need to succeed while maintaining the new boundary that pee and poop only belong in the potty, and most of all, no more diapers!

POWER STRUGGLES & POTTY RESISTANCE

I have yet to hear of a toddler who hasn't pushed the limits or thrown a tantrum when they didn't get their way. There's a great reason for this! Around the age of two, children begin to crave independence and autonomy. And guess what, when you pair that up with potty training, sometimes it's a power struggle just waiting to happen.

In psychology, there is a theory known as the Premack Principle that puts it all into perspective. This principle states that a person is likely to perform an undesirable behavior in order to have access to something more desirable.

The Premack Principle

Also known as the "relativity theory of reinforcement" or the "first/then rule." This psychological theory states that a person is likely to perform an undesirable behavior in order to have access to something more desirable.

Having accidents in their underwear, refusing to sit on the potty, or acting out about potty use in general is an undesirable behavior to your child. They don't necessarily WANT to do those things, but it can potentially lead to getting their diapers back, getting extra attention from you, or avoiding having to change their routine or step outside their comfort zone, which are all desirable to them.

Most likely, a child who is having these struggles with potty training is not going to use the potty simply to appease you or because you ask them to. Instead, there has to be something in it for them. Every child has a motivator (such as candy, toys, a special activity, TV time, staying up late, etc.), you just have to find out what it is. Maybe they won't go on the potty for a piece of chocolate, but they will in order to get tablet time. Find out their motivator and use it as a bargaining tool to get the behavior you want (like using the potty). This way, you both come out satisfied!

Example: If you want to watch your TV show, you have to use the potty correctly first.

In this case, the less desirable behavior of using the potty is getting them access to the more desirable behavior of watching TV.

When you encounter these power struggles after you're certain that your child knows what to do when it comes to using the potty but they continue to choose not to, you

WE ARE REALLY STRUGGLING. SHOULD WE TAKE A BREAK?

When you encounter a lot of struggles during potty training and you feel like there aren't many successes to speak of, or maybe things seem to be getting worse instead of better, it often leads you to question your child's actual readiness and makes you want to take a break and try again later. Before you decide to stop or keep going, see if any of these things that would indicate a lack of emotional readiness for potty training apply to your child:

- A seemingly genuine fear of the potty itself. Kicking, screaming, clinging in order to not sit.
- A seemingly genuine fear of peeing/pooping without a diaper on.
- Being upset as they're peeing or pooping, or trying to stop themselves from going.
- Extreme withholding behaviors, such as not releasing for several hours, when they need to go.
- Little or no success in the potty after a four to five day attempt.

If ANY of these items are present, it is probably a good idea to press pause and go back to diapers temporarily. Remember, this is not a reflection on you! Emotional readiness is one of those things that is super hard to predict, and sometimes, you can never tell until you actually dive in and get started. Taking a break is not failing. You can always come back to things later when your child has a chance to emotionally mature a little bit more!

Some things are more behavioral and don't necessarily warrant taking a break, unless of course, they are affecting your own mental health or your relationship with your child. These could include:

- Having a clear understanding of what the potty is for and having used the potty successfully, but sometimes refusing to do so.
- Having accidents at "choice" times, such as when they don't want to stop playing or in order to get your attention.
- Having tantrums surrounding potty use despite having used the potty successfully before.

Potty training is notoriously known for creating power struggles, so when you find yourself encountering behavior issues, don't feel guilty about setting clear, consistent boundaries and pushing forward. Sticking to your commitment is going to be the main solution to get things back on track.

WITHHOLDING

In the early stages of potty training, it can be fairly common for children to pee and poop less while they are learning their body cues. Sometimes, this can be pretty worrisome to us as parents – especially when it seems to go on for hours and you're wondering how they can possibly be holding it that long! Typically, it's just a temporary adjustment to their normal potty routine and not something to worry about.

However, there are times where children do withhold pee and poop out of fear or resistance to using the potty. This may look like not peeing for very long periods of time (generally several hours or more) to the point of pain or discomfort or trying to physically hold back from releasing pee or poop when they really need to go. This could look like putting their hand over their bottom, crossing their legs when they feel pee coming, holding in their pee or poop until bedtime when they get access to a pullup, or holding it in until they simply can't hold it in anymore and, literally, burst.

Children resort to withholding behaviors for various reasons, such as fear of the changes that come with potty training or out of a desire to experiment with independence and autonomy through power struggles. The stubbornness of, "I'm absolutely not going to poop until you give me that diaper back!" can become very real. They aren't peeing or pooping on that potty and you can't make them!

No matter what the reason for their withholding is, it is stressful and frustrating. You may even wonder if they will experience physical harm from withholding. Don't worry though, there are ways to help your child overcome these tendencies.

When those physical signs and behavior changes of needing to go potty become more apparent, try to remove some of the pressure and stress and make the process as fun as you can, so no matter what their reasoning is for not releasing on the potty, they at least will be super motivated to give it a try!

Tips to help your child release on the potty:

- Fill up a basket with new sensory toys that you know your child will love playing with and only have them accessible during potty time. Sensory toys are less stimulating than electronic devices so it could help to distract your child while relaxing them enough to release.

- Offer appropriate choices. Choices are always a great way for your child to feel a certain level of control in an otherwise uncertain time. Let them choose how to make the environment more comfortable. Think things like: lights on or off? Privacy or company? Sit on the toilet backwards or forwards? Sing a song or blow some bubbles?

- Speaking of blowing bubbles – this is a GREAT way for your child to relax and release their bladder and bowels. It doesn't have to be just blowing bubbles. It could be a pinwheel, a toy trumpet, or blowing through a straw into a glass of milk. The act of blowing mimics deep breathing which helps to relax the pelvic floor.

- Break out the water play! Placing your child's feet into a small tub of warm water while they sit on the potty can help to release their bladder. It can also be a fun distraction for them while they sit. They can "wash" toy cars or play with toy sharks in the water. It's like a kind of potty sensory bin!

- Stickers on the toes. Give your child a sheet of stickers while sitting on the potty and ask them to put a sticker on each of their toes. The bending over action can actually help massage the abdomen making it easier to pee or poop.

- Magic potty drops. I learned this trick from my labor and delivery nurse after I had my son. A drop or two of peppermint oil in the toilet bowl before sitting down can trigger bladder release! I gave birth in a very busy hospital and they needed those birthing rooms. But you can't be released to recovery until you've peed! She would use this trick to help women be able to go faster and easier, and it can work during potty training too.

But what if none of these tips or tricks work? I encourage parents to give a solid try for at least three full days to see if the withholding behaviors improve before deciding to take a break from potty training. Extreme withholding, for 12 hours or more for pee or three days or more for poop, can potentially lead to physical problems. Above all else, we always want to prioritize health and safety.

Lastly, always listen to your gut. If it truly feels wrong to keep going, then it probably is. You can always take some time off to let your child start peeing and pooping normally again and then revisit the potty training process later.

POOP PROBLEMS

One of the most common problems I've seen parents face is getting their children to poop in the potty. In one poll I performed among more than 300 parents, over 40% of them admitted to struggling with this issue. So if this seems to be you, know you're not alone.

Even if your child is doing really well with peeing on the potty, every poop might be an accident. That's okay. Learning how to poop in the potty can take a lot longer to master because there are a lot fewer opportunities to practice! Think about it – your child probably poops once for every five to ten pees. So in theory, it could take five to ten times longer for your child to learn how to poop on the potty.

Pooping on the potty can take longer for a child to master because there are fewer opportunities to practice! While these accidents are frustrating, remember to bring your calm and patience to the situation so you don't accidentally create negative connotations around pooping!

Pooping in the potty versus pooping in a diaper is a very different sensation that can be hard for a lot of kids to come to terms with. When they poop in their diaper (or underwear), the poop comes out and stays right up against their body. When they poop into the potty, the poop falls out and away from their body, which can be pretty darn scary! It's just so different, and there are a lot of things happening from a sensory standpoint that might be making it difficult for your child to poop on the potty.

Sometimes, this leads to them withholding their poop altogether. This, in turn, can lead to constipation, which can lead to pain or discomfort during pooping, which can lead to more withholding, and then the vicious cycle continues.

If you notice that three or more days have passed without a poop, give your child's doctor a call and see what they recommend for constipation alleviation and prevention. Typically offering a stool softener, probiotics, fiber supplement, or an osmotic laxative can help get things moving again.

Since pooping on the potty is such a major thing for some kids to tackle, do your best to offer lots of choices so they feel in control, help them feel as comfortable as possible while they're trying to go, and offer a super cool reward for successes. Avoid giving up too soon or just offering your child a diaper for pooping because they are requesting it. There are plenty of ways to work through this obstacle, and I've outlined them all in my affordable online course, *How to Get Your Child to Poop on the Potty: The Advanced Guide*. If you're finding the poop struggles are persisting for more than a few days, hop over to that course to get a plan in place. The sooner the better!

REGRESSIONS

Say your child has been doing great with using the potty. They no longer need reminders, they are pooping consistently, and they're even sometimes staying dry overnight! Life is good. Then, out of nowhere, it's one accident after another, and it seems like everything they previously learned went out the window! This is what would be classified as a potty training regression.

A regression, in any aspect, is when a child reverts back to a previous stage of behavior or development. Regressions are usually observed when kids are feeling emotional stress as a result of some sort of disruption to their regular routine. Young children can't always express their emotions clearly, so instead, they may regress to a time where they remember feeling more safe and secure as a way to seek comfort or extra attention from you – kind of like a defense mechanism. For many children, safety and security comes through the intimacy of being changed by their parent or caregiver, and that can lead to them having more potty accidents.

Mindset shift!

Children almost never start having potty accidents again with ill intentions. Always rule out a medical cause first, but almost always, a potty training regression is a child's way of saying, "Help me. I'm feeling out of sorts and I need extra love and attention right now!"

These regressions can come in the form of having more accidents during the day, no longer self-initiating potty use, wetting themselves during nap or nighttime when they were previously dry, or no longer pooping in the potty. No matter how it presents itself, it obviously leads to a lot of frustration and uncertainty as a parent. But, potty training regressions are fairly common. That said, it doesn't make it any less difficult or stressful for either you or your child. Do your best to remain positive, consistent, and offer them some extra love. Most regressions will only last about two weeks or less, and before you know it, they'll be back to using the potty reliably again.

If you're interested in learning more on how to prevent and correct potty training regressions, be sure to check out my online mini-course, *How to Deal: Potty Training Regressions*.

NO SELF-INITIATION

Another super common struggle you might encounter during the potty learning process is a lack of self initiation. This might look like your child not telling you when they have to go potty, which ends up resulting in an accident every time. It's understandably frustrating when your child isn't seemingly able to listen to their body and take themselves to sit on the potty. It probably makes you feel like you're the one who is potty trained, as in: you're trained on when to take your child to the potty to prevent an accident. That's not how it should be!

That said though, self-initiation can sometimes be one of the last things to click into place for some kids, especially if they have a speech or communication delay. We have to remember that progress and successes look different for everyone, and if, for right now, your success looks like your child going potty on a schedule, or you reading your child's cues and taking them to the potty, then that is perfectly okay! Some kids self-initiate really quickly, while others take up to four weeks or more before they make the first move on their own. Some children who have certain disabilities or are neurodiverse might never have the ability to self-initiate.

We've already talked about being careful not to over prompt your child or take them to sit on the potty at set time intervals which can really slow this part of the process down. Remember – the goal is for your child to learn what a full bladder feels like so it gets a chance to send a signal to the brain saying, "Take me to the potty, I need emptying!" If they are being taken to sit before their bladder is actually full, that bladder-to-brain connection doesn't get a chance to develop properly and, even worse, it can fool the bladder into thinking it needs emptying when it isn't even full yet – therefore resulting in more accidents. So, while it may seem counterintuitive initially to let your child have accidents, those accidents are actually when the most critical part of learning is occurring. They allow your child to learn their body urges much more quickly than preventing accidents at all costs and taking your child to the bathroom at set times. Learning their urges is how self-initiation begins. Not to mention, over prompting can annoy and frustrate your child with the potty process leading to more power struggles and resistance.

If your child is really struggling with telling you they need to go, do your best to help them recognize their body's cues when you notice them. For example, if you see your child dancing around like they need to pee but they aren't making the move to go to the potty on their own, say, "Hey, I can see that you've got some wiggles. That's your body telling you it's potty time! Come on, let's go sit." After practicing this a few times, you can start engaging them more by saying, "I'm noticing the wiggles again! What's your body telling you?" Let them start to take more and more responsibility while empowering them and offering that encouragement.

Additionally, offering occasional reminders can help your child be more successful with their potty use. This is different from actually prompting them to go sit on the potty at a particular time because you are simply tossing out a reminder when they're in the middle of an activity and it might be time for them to pee or poop soon. Just say, "Hey, remember, when you need to go potty, it's right here. Let's keep our pants dry." Keeping the idea fresh in their busy little heads can ease them into the responsibility of doing it all on their own every time.

If your child struggles with self-initiation when you're out and about – practice makes perfect. Make a point to visit bathrooms when you first arrive in a new place so your child gets familiar with the idea that there are bathrooms everywhere you go, and they don't need to just hold it and then eventually have an accident. You can even give them a choice by bringing a travel potty along in the car. "If you need to go potty, just let me know and we can use this one here in the store, or we can go out to the car."

For more prolonged struggles with self initiation, or if your child has unique needs or a disability, be sure to reach out for a consultation to get some customized support!

chapter twelve

you've got this

The Learning Continues...

I'VE SAID IT BEFORE, AND I'LL SAY IT AGAIN - POTTY TRAINING IS A PROCESS, NOT A ONE TIME EVENT.

While you will likely be seeing some really good progress after the first few days or weeks, keep in mind that the teaching and reinforcing of these new skills is far from over. It's perfectly normal to see the occasional accident here and there for months, or sometimes years, to come. As long as the accidents aren't happening frequently, and you aren't noticing a pattern developing that could indicate a regression, take them in stride and know that each mistake is a learning opportunity.

Here are some ways to continue to set your child up for potty success:

- Offer reminders about using the potty when accidents are more likely such as when they are sick, overly excited, or anxious.
- Check in with how their body is feeling when they've been doing an activity that might have their mind too stimulated or distracted to be thinking about the potty and recommend potty breaks as needed.
- Keep a travel potty with you for longer than you think you might need it just to make sure your child has the option in an emergency situation.

Potty training progress isn't always linear and it is going to look different for every child depending on a number of different factors. As long as the steps forward are aligning with your family's goals, that is all that matters.

The Hidden Benefits of Potty Training

In case you are still on the fence about starting, there are a lot of great benefits that come along with potty training which might not be quite as obvious as ditching the diapers.

As you navigate the jungles of potty training, you'll be gathering skills that you can apply in other parenting situations as well. The new knowledge you've gained from this experience can be utilized and built upon as your child continues to grow!

A DEEPER UNDERSTANDING

Throughout the potty training process, you've likely learned a lot about your child that you didn't know before:

- Their personality type
- How they handle change
- Their learning style
- What motivates them
- Certain preferences
- Sensory sensitivities
- Power struggle triggers

These things all become more apparent as you help guide your child through this major life milestone. You'll likely find yourself remembering what you've learned about caring for and interacting with your child through potty training the next time they are tackling a new skill.

Knowing your child's inner workings is only going to further deepen the bond you share with them.

CAREGIVER COMMUNICATION

In addition to learning more about your child, you've learned how to communicate with your child's care team more effectively. There has likely been communication among a lot of people to keep the potty a consistent and positive concept in your child's life across all different environments. As a mom myself, I can tell you, this is only the beginning! There are many years of interactions with future teachers, coaches, babysitters, friends, and family still to come. Know that the more involved you are, and the more you keep the lines of communication open and honest, the better care your child will receive.

THINKING POSITIVE

I hope that after reading this book, you've learned a thing or two about the power of positive thinking. I encourage you to carry that forward - not just in parenting, but in all aspects of life. Continue to look for any small progress or success and focus on the good. As Willie Nelson once said, "Once you replace negative thoughts with positive ones, you'll start having positive results." Amen, Willie.

Contact Information

Email:
info@pottytrainingconsultant.com

Website:
www.pottytrainingconsultant.com

I'LL LEAVE YOU WITH THIS...

Never ever forget that you were chosen to be your child's parent, and deep down, you know what is best for them. Please don't make potty training a competition or compare your journey to anyone else's - it will be your child's and theirs alone.

If, at any point, you feel like you need additional support, please know that myself and my team are here for you. We are passionate about helping families say goodbye to diapers and make potty training a positive and successful experience, and we have consultation options to fit every budget. Don't hesitate to reach out so we can work alongside you to meet your goals. Asking for help shows strength, not weakness.

Happy Pottying!
xoxo

Made in United States
Troutdale, OR
05/20/2024